WHEN THE CHURCH IS SCATTERED

Discipling In-Person and Virtual Worshippers Into a Unified Body of Christ

DR. BARBARA A. ROSS

www.TrueVinePublishing.org

When the Church is Scattered
Dr. Barbara A. Ross

Published by
True Vine Publishing Co.
810 Dominican Dr.
Nashville, TN 37228
www.TrueVinePublishing.org

ISBN: 978-1-968092-79-5 Paperback
ISBN: 978-1-968092-80-1 eBook

Printed in the United States of America—First printing.

DEDICATION

I gratefully dedicate this work to my three sons: Wayne, Orlando and (In Memory of Wendell). I also dedicate this work to my late father and Mother, and to all of my siblings. Finally, I dedicate this work to the late Dr. Kimberly S. Credit, with much love and deep admiration. With the utmost gratitude, awe, and thanksgiving, I compassionately devote this study to the DuPage African Methodist Episcopal (AME) Church, located in Lisle, Illinois

ACKNOWLEDGMENTS

To my mentors, Dr. Donnell J. Moore, the late Dr. Kimberly S. Credit, and Dr. Ralph D. West, I wholeheartedly thank you for your wisdom, leadership, direction, and support. Dr. Moore, your unwavering willingness to lead with empathy, compassion, and courage helped to undergird me through my days of uncertainties and unplanned challenges. Namely, the untimely sudden death of our beloved Dr. Kimberly S. Credit resulted in uncertainty and unplanned challenges. Her death was a punch in the center of my being, and going through the grieving process was hard. You were there right with me and have been a visionary coach and leader in my life.

Dr. Moore, you and the entire faculty and staff of Payne Theological Seminary have been exemplary steady, steering guides and comforters. You have allowed the Holy Spirit to lead and guide you, not only concerning me, but also the entire student body. You are great leaders who have dedicated your life, assistance, and ministry experience to the service of building the Kingdom of God.

TABLE OF CONTENTS

INTRODUCTION

The church is changing. Across the world, congregations have faced challenges that few could have anticipated. The COVID-19 pandemic disrupted not only how people gathered, but how they connected, worshipped, and experienced community. What once felt stable and familiar was suddenly uncertain. Doors closed, sanctuaries emptied and ministries were forced to adapt in real time.

Yet in the middle of that disruption, something unexpected happened. People still showed up in a different space. They logged in. They participated in worship, Bible studies, and conversations from their homes, their cars, and wherever they could find space to connect. A new kind of church participant emerged. These were not always the traditional, in-person members. These were individuals who may never have walked through the physical doors of the church, yet they were present, engaged, and spiritually hungry.

This shift was not gradual. It was sudden. It was what I refer to as "The Pandemic Push." The Pandemic Push forced churches into a new reality almost overnight. Leaders had to make quick decisions with little guidance. Congregations had to adjust without preparation. Churches everywhere were trying to survive, to remain connected, and to continue serving their communities in the midst of uncertainty.

In the process, many churches unintentionally created a divide. Those who gathered in person remained at the center of decision-making, relationships, and activities. Meanwhile, those who engaged virtually were often left on the margins. Not because they lacked commitment, but because the church had not yet fully adapted to include them. They were present, but not always recognized; participating, but not always integrated.

This was not done out of exclusion or ill intent. It was the result of rapid change, limited understanding, and the overwhelming pressure to respond to a global crisis. Still, the result is real. There are now two expressions of the church operating at the same time: those who gather physically and those who gather virtually. The question is no longer whether both groups exist. The question is how the church responds to both in a way that reflects unity, purpose, and the heart of Christ.

This book emerges from that tension. It is rooted in real ministry experience within a local church context, but it speaks to a broader reality facing churches everywhere. It explores what it means to disciple, engage, and unify both in-person and virtual worshippers into one body.

The goal is not simply to adapt to change, but to understand it. The church has always been called to make disciples. That calling has not changed. What has changed is the environment in which that calling is carried out. This moment invites the church to rethink how it builds relationships, fosters belonging, and creates pathways for spiritual growth for everyone who shows up, regardless of how they show up.

The church is not confined to a building. It is a body, and if the body is to function as one, then every member must be seen, valued, and connected. This book is an invitation to reconsider how we do that in a scattered world.

CHAPTER ONE

Ministry Focus

The synergy between my spiritual autobiography and my understanding of the church in its present context has not only transformed my life, but it has also shaped the message of this book.

I was born in the year of 1960, along with my fraternal twin sister, to my parents, the late Mr. Willard David Ross, Sr. and Mrs. Mary Jean Tolbert Ross. I arrived three minutes before my twin and was the eighth of fifteen children. My father was born during the year of the Great Mississippi River Flood of 1927, one of the most devastating floods in the history of the United States. His family lived in the Mississippi Delta, one of the hardest-hit areas. In order to survive, they had to stay on top of their house for days until help arrived. His mother was pregnant with him at the time. Had she not survived, our family line would have ended there.

My father worked tirelessly to provide for his family. When he was not working on the Ross Family Land, he often worked multiple jobs. He spent many years at the Oil Mill in Hollandale and Greenville, Mississippi. He was also a veteran who served in World War II and received an honorable discharge from the United States Army. He was a man of faith who confessed hope in Christ at an early age and remained connected to the church throughout his life.

My great grandfather, Reverend Armstead Ross, Sr., was a Baptist minister who was widely respected in the community. He was both a farmer and a businessman. He owned land, raised livestock, hunted for food, and operated a grits mill. He was known for his intelligence, his discipline, and his ability to provide. His life demonstrated what it meant to build something that could sustain not only a family, but a community.

My mother, Mary Jean Tolbert Ross, was the oldest of ninth siblings. She accepted Jesus Christ as her Lord and Savior at an early age and faithfully served in the church for over fifty years. She sang in the choir, served on the Mother Board, and lived out her faith through both her service and her work. Her career included nursing and teaching, and she even owned her own boutique, where her motto was, "Christ is the Answer."

I grew up on the Ross family land, which had been passed down through generations as heir property. This meant the land was not to be sold, but preserved for future generations. Life on the Ross family land required work, discipline, and resourcefulness. We raised animals, planted crops, and made many of the things we needed to survive.

My childhood was filled with experiences that, even then, felt unusual. One morning, at about three years old, I noticed something in the chimney while my mother was combing my hair. There was a fire in the chimney. Not smoke from the fireplace, but an actual fire. I told my mother, but she was rushing to get to work and did not stop to check. Later that day, when my parents returned home, the house had burned to the ground. There were no nearby neighbors and no phones to call for help. Over the years, our family would experience multiple house fires.

At five or six years old, I would put my hands outside the window to catch the rain. One day, my hand was struck by lightning. I never told anyone. At eight years old, a pot of boiling water spilled on me, burning me from my stomach down to my feet. I ran outside and jumped into a barrel of cool water, which likely prevented the burns from becoming even worse.

At nine or ten years old, I saw a large tornado approaching our home. I ran inside to warn my mother. Later that day, the news reported the damage it had caused in nearby areas.

Looking back, I can see how God's hand was present, even when I did not fully understand it. At around twelve years old, I made the decision to join Mt. Zion Missionary Baptist Church. This decision came during a weeklong revival in our neighborhood. Each night, I found myself on the mourner's bench, seeking the presence of the Holy Spirit. No one could fully explain what that experience would feel like. On the final night, when the Spirit came upon me, it felt like a wave of warmth. That night, I gave the preacher my hand and God my heart.

In July 1972, I was baptized in Deer Creek by Reverend A. D. Williams on a hot Sunday morning. Soon after, I joined the choir and became a committed member. One Sunday, while singing, I felt the Holy Spirit move so strongly that it seemed as though I was not singing alone. The atmosphere in the church shifted. People were shouting, crying, and praising God. Even my sister later told me that something was different about me that day.

At fifteen, I felt led to bring other children to church. I went from house to house inviting them. To my surprise, they all came. I had never driven before, but I attempted to drive my parents' station wagon to take them. My father stopped me, but instead of punishing me, he got dressed and drove us himself. Not only that, he continued to take us to church for many Sundays afterward.

Years later, in July 1983, I moved to Chicago in search of a better life and to further my education. After some time, I realized something was missing. I needed a church home.

I initially attended a Baptist church, but while sitting in the service, I clearly heard the Holy Spirit telling me that church was not where I was meant to be. There was confusion in the atmosphere, and I discerned that it was not the place for me. I never returned.

The following Sunday, I went to Grant Memorial AME Church, located in Chicago, Illinois. No one invited me. I had never heard of it before. Yet, I knew I was led there by the Holy Spirit. It was there that I would eventually answer the call to preach.

That calling did not come easily. In July 1989, after many sleepless nights and moments of wrestling with God, I finally said, "Yes, Lord, here I am. Send me; I will go." That moment marked a turning point in my life.

Over time, I was licensed to preach and later ordained as both an Itinerant Deacon and an Itinerant Elder in the African Methodist Episcopal Church. I began the work of ministry, including organizing a new church that started as a Bible study and eventually grew into a congregation.

Life, however, was not without challenges. I experienced personal transitions, including divorce and frequent moves. During one of those seasons, in July 2004, I had a dream. In the dream, I heard the Holy Spirit say, "Naperville, Naperville."

When I woke up, I questioned why Naperville. I did not know anyone there. Still, I followed what I believed God was telling me to do. I relocated to Naperville, Illinois, even though it required commuting long distances.

Later, while driving, I saw a sign that read, "While the building is under construction, the church will meet in City Hall." At that moment, I understood. The first "Naperville" was for me. The second was for me to move the church to Naperville.

I began searching for a place for the church to meet, which led to a three- to four-month struggle with the city. I was told that religious groups were not allowed to use public meeting spaces. I persisted.

What I did not know at the time was that the situation had drawn public attention. A local newspaper followed the story, a lawyer from the Citizen Advocacy Center, located in Elmhurst, Illinois, read what the city counsel was putting me through and wrote a letter stating that the city's policy was unconstitutional and violated the First Amendment.

After months of resistance, there was a breakthrough. On December 18, 2005, the policy was changed. Religious groups were granted access to public meeting spaces. The front page of the newspaper featured the victory, with a picture of me, with my right arm raised, and the caption, "Praises at the Dias."

I take no credit for that victory. It was the work of God. This experience affirmed something I have come to believe deeply. When we take our calling seriously, remain faithful, and trust God, He will move in ways we cannot orchestrate on our own.

As my journey continued, I served in multiple churches across different regions and denominations. Each experience shaped my understanding of ministry, leadership, and discipleship.

Education also played a critical role in my development. As Nelson Mandela once said, "Education is the most powerful weapon which you can use to change the world." He also noted that when a good head and a good heart are combined with the ability to communicate, something powerful is created.

Education allows us to understand the world, to think critically, and to engage with different perspectives. It connects us to the broader human experience and prepares us to respond to the challenges of our time.

My own educational journey began in Mississippi and continued in Chicago, where I earned degrees in business, theology, and spiritual formation. I later pursued doctoral studies, focusing on transformational preaching. Throughout this process, I recognized that education is not just about knowledge. It is about preparation for purpose.

This brings us to the context in which this book was developed. DuPage African Methodist Episcopal Church, located in Lisle, Illinois, provides the setting for much of this work. Its mission is to minister to the spiritual, intellectual, physical, emotional, and environmental needs of all people by sharing the Gospel through both word and action.

The church has served its community for decades, offering outreach programs, leadership development, and opportunities for spiritual growth. It is a vibrant congregation with a strong foundation and a commitment to service.

However, like many churches, it faced a significant challenge during the COVID-19 pandemic.

When the pandemic began, the church was forced to move to a fully virtual platform almost overnight. This shift revealed a deeper issue. New "virtual members" were being added, but they were not always fully included or integrated into the life of the church.

Churches everywhere were facing the same struggle. Leaders were trying to figure out how to maintain connection, how to make virtual disciples effectively, and how to function in a world where physical gathering was no longer guaranteed. There was confusion, urgency, and, in many cases, panic.

The pandemic did not just disrupt the church. It exposed what needed to change. It became clear to me that discipleship could no longer be confined to the four walls of a building. The church had been pushed outside, whether it was ready or not.

This led me to a realization: If the church is to survive and remain effective, it must find new ways to make disciples. It must learn how to connect, relate, and engage in ways that reflect the current reality. It must be willing to let go of methods that no longer serve the mission.

During this time, I began to say, "Think outside the box… and then think outside of that box."

The pandemic created a new reality that requires deeper thinking and greater adaptability. The church must go further than it has before. Jesus' command remains the same:

"Go therefore and make disciples of all nations…" (Matthew 28:19, NRSV)

This is not optional. It is the mandate of the church. As Donald Hagner observed, this passage serves as a summary of the major themes of Matthew's Gospel and stands as one of the most significant charges given by Jesus.

Therefore, I propose that if the church begins to intentionally include and engage these new, non-traditional members, they will become active participants in the life of the church. The church will grow, both spiritually and numerically. Resources will increase, but more importantly, disciples will be made.

And in all of this, God will receive the glory.

CHAPTER TWO

Ministry Foundations I

This chapter explores literature, systems, and models of ministry that help move the church's disciple-making efforts from older, traditional approaches into methods that better reflect the world we live in today. It focuses on research, ministry models, and real examples that offer practical ways to include members—especially those who participate virtually—into the life of the church and into a deeper relationship with Christ.

At its core, the assignment has not changed. Jesus made it clear in Matthew 28:19: *"Go therefore and make disciples of all nations…"* The question is not whether the church should make disciples. The question is how that calling is lived out in a world that looks very different from the one many of our current methods were built for.

The pandemic forced a shift. What once felt optional became necessary. Churches had to learn how to function beyond physical walls, and in doing so, many discovered both new opportunities and new challenges. That shift revealed something important: disciple-making must be flexible enough to meet people where they are, including in digital spaces.

Meredith Gould, in *The Social Media Gospel*, helps frame this reality. She describes social media as a space where conversations are created, relationships are formed, and communities are sustained. Rather than replacing traditional ministry, these platforms extend it. They allow the church to remain present in the everyday lives of people in ways that were not previously possible.

That idea of presence is critical. Ministry has always been about connection. Social media simply changes the location of that connection.

Gordon Comer, in *Soul Whisperer*, challenges the church to rethink how it approaches evangelism altogether. He points out that many traditional methods no longer connect with people in meaningful ways. Instead of relying on one-size-fits-all approaches, he emphasizes the importance of conversation; real dialogue that meets people where they are and takes the time to understand what they believe and why.

Jesus modeled this well. He did not approach every person the same way. He engaged individuals differently, spoke into their specific situations, and built relationships before expecting transformation. That model still works. The difference is that many of those conversations are now happening in virtual spaces.

Programs like the *30-Day Evangelism Challenge* show how this can be done in practical ways. This initiative uses short, daily video content and social media engagement to help everyday believers grow more confident in sharing their faith. Over time, participants begin to move past fear and into action, not through pressure, but through consistent exposure and practice. It is simple, accessible, and effective, especially in a world where people are already spending significant time online.

The lesson is clear: disciple-making does not always require something new. Sometimes it requires presenting timeless truth in a format people can actually engage with.

History shows that this kind of adaptation is not new. In *The Awakening Coast*, the work of Moravian missionaries in Nicaragua demonstrates how faith can take root when it is presented in ways that connect with people's lived experiences. Over time, what began as an outside influence became deeply embedded in the culture, shaping both spiritual life and community structure.

The success of that movement was not accidental. It was contextual. The message did not change, but the approach did. That same principle applies today.

The idea of church itself is also expanding. In *A Church Without Walls*, the concept of online church is explored as more than a temporary solution. It is presented as a real extension of community. Drawing from interpretive community theory, the study shows that people understand and experience meaning within the context of shared beliefs and relationships, whether those relationships exist in physical spaces or virtual ones.

In other words, community is not defined by location. It is defined by connection. This became especially clear during COVID-19. Churches around the world had to quickly adapt, often using whatever tools were available. As Bryson, Andres, and Davies describe in their work on virtual church services, homes became places of worship. Living rooms became sanctuaries. The line between sacred and everyday space began to blur.

For many, this shift was uncomfortable. For others, it was freeing. People who may not have attended a physical service found themselves engaging online. Others who were once limited by distance, health, or circumstance were suddenly able to participate consistently. The church, in many ways, became more accessible.

This pattern of growth during disruption is not unique to the pandemic. Catherine Wanner's work on evangelical communities in the former Soviet Union shows how faith can flourish in times of transition. When barriers shift, new opportunities often emerge.

The challenge is recognizing those opportunities and responding to them. Paul Borden speaks directly to this in *Assaulting the Gates*. He argues that churches often desire change but attempt it in small, incomplete ways. Real transformation requires a shift in mindset. It requires leadership, strategy, and a willingness to move beyond comfort.

That shift is not just structural. It is relational. Efforts to grow the church must remain rooted in authentic relationships. Studies on congregational life consistently show that people stay connected not simply because of programs, but because of how they are treated and how they experience community. Loving relationships, practiced consistently, create environments where people feel seen, valued, and welcomed.

This becomes even more important in virtual spaces, where connection can easily become transactional if it is not intentional. Technology, however, continues to shape how connection happens. Works like *From Social Butterfly to Engaged Citizen* highlight how virtual platforms have created more participatory environments. People are no longer passive consumers. They are active participants, contributing, responding, and engaging in real time.

The church must recognize this shift. Discipleship can no longer be limited to one-directional teaching. It must become interactive, ongoing, and relational.

This is where virtual outreach becomes essential. Social media platforms, websites, podcasts, and video content are not just tools for visibility. They are spaces for ministry. They allow the church to reach across geographic, cultural, and social boundaries. They make it possible to connect with individuals who may never walk through the doors of a physical building.

As Moses Mwicigi suggests, these platforms are no longer optional. They are needed to reach the masses globally. An online presence through social media and cyberchurch is a must to expand the Kingdom and give glory to God. Social media is no longer a tool used to increase the "brick and mortar" ministry; it is the ocean in which all ministries must sink or swim. It is key to the church reaching millions of people over the internet, and crucial in receiving feedback from millions of people across the world.

Examples of this can be seen in churches that have embraced online ministry. Virtual services have reached audiences far beyond local congregations. Messages are shared globally. Worship is experienced across time zones.

Music, in particular, has played a powerful role in maintaining connection. As highlighted in *Ways to Help Keep The Church Members Connected*, rotating worship leaders, sharing recorded services, and creating engaging online experiences have helped people stay connected even when they could not be physically present. One participant described worshiping from home, still able to praise, still able to feel connected, even while sitting in their own living room.

That kind of access matters. It reminds us that worship is not confined to a building. It is an experience that can travel. At the same time, the church must remain aware of those who exist on the margins. The work on *Mission on the Margins* challenges us to consider who may be overlooked in traditional models of ministry. The pandemic revealed gaps, but it also opened doors to new ways of reaching and serving people. In many ways, the movement of church into homes and virtual spaces has created new opportunities to center voices that were previously unheard.

This raises important questions for the future. What does it mean to be the church in a virtual age? How do we maintain authenticity, authority, and connection in spaces that are constantly changing? How do we ensure that the message remains clear while the methods continue to evolve?

These are not easy questions, but they are necessary ones. History shows that the church has always adapted. From early movements to global missions, from physical gatherings to virtual communities, the method has changed many times. The mission has not.

The responsibility now is to continue that pattern, to remain rooted in truth while being responsive to the world around us. The church is not disappearing. It is shifting. The question is whether we are willing to shift with it.

CHAPTER THREE

Ministry Foundations II

The work of discipleship does not begin with new ideas. It begins with understanding what has already been said, what has already been lived, and what has already been revealed through Scripture and through the voices of those who have gone before us. Throughout history, theologians, pastors, and leaders have wrestled with the same questions the church faces today. What does it mean to make disciples? How do we remain faithful to Scripture while responding to the realities of our current context?

The impact of COVID-19 forced the global church into a new way of thinking about these questions. A new form of disciple-making emerged, one that extended beyond physical buildings and into virtual spaces. This shift did not change the mission of the church, but it did change how that mission is carried out. As a result, the church must now consider how to respond to this new harvest of people who have been drawn into the life of the church through virtual means.

One of the greatest challenges facing the church today is not a lack of opportunity, but a resistance to change. Many churches struggle to let go of familiar methods in order to embrace new ones. This resistance limits the church's ability to reach and disciple those who are already present but not fully integrated into the life of the church.

Traditionally, churches have relied on their existing members to carry out the work of ministry. The same individuals serve, lead, and participate, while others remain on the outside looking in. However, the shift brought on by the pandemic has introduced a new group of people—those who are connected to the church but not in the traditional sense.

These "non-traditional members" are not necessarily absent. In many ways, they are present in greater numbers than ever before. They attend virtual worship services, participate in Bible studies, give financially, and engage with the life of the church from a distance. Some have never set foot inside a church building, yet they consider themselves part of the church community.

This reality challenges the church to rethink what it means to be a member. The term "non-traditional" can no longer be limited to those outside the church. In this new environment, even those who have long been considered traditional members are now participating in non-traditional ways. The line between member and non-member has become less defined, and the church must now respond to this shift with intentionality.

The opportunity before the church is significant. If leaders are willing to rethink how ministry is structured, they can begin to incorporate these non-traditional members into the life of the church in meaningful ways. Service ministries, for example, can become a bridge for engagement. By inviting individuals to use their gifts and talents in service, the church creates pathways for connection, growth, and ultimately discipleship.

When the church limits itself to only those who are already fully integrated, it misses the opportunity to make new disciples. But when it expands its vision, it begins to see the potential in those who have been drawn into the church through unexpected means.

This is not a new problem. Throughout history, the church has faced challenges related to discipleship. From the early church to the structured movements of John Wesley, from the theological systems of John Calvin to the liberative theology of James Cone, the question of how to form and sustain disciples has always been present. Each of these voices approached discipleship within their own context, yet all recognized that it required intentional formation, not passive participation.

Dietrich Bonhoeffer, in *The Cost of Discipleship*, offered one of the clearest warnings against reducing discipleship to something shallow. He wrote, "Cheap grace is the grace we bestow on ourselves… grace without discipleship, grace without the cross, grace without Jesus Christ." His words still confront the modern church. Discipleship cannot be reduced to a moment or a label. It must involve transformation.

Today, however, discipleship has often been reduced to a moment rather than a process. In many churches, becoming a disciple is equated with making a profession of faith and receiving baptism. After that, individuals are often left to navigate their faith on their own. This reflects a broader cultural tendency toward individualism, where people are encouraged to function independently rather than within a community.

The early church operated differently. New believers, known as catechumens, entered into a structured process of discipleship that often lasted several years. They were immersed in teaching, trained in the fundamentals of the faith, and guided in their spiritual growth. Discipleship was not a one-time event. It was a continuous journey of transformation.

At the center of this journey is the Great Commission found in Matthew 28:18–20. Jesus declares that all authority in heaven and on earth has been given to Him and commands His followers to make disciples of all nations. This command is not limited to a specific group or time. It extends to the entire church.

The Great Commission is not simply about going. It is about making disciples through a process that includes baptizing and teaching. These actions are not separate from disciple-making; they are the means by which disciples are formed.

This passage also reveals something deeper about the nature of God's mission. The mission of the church is not something that originates with us. It originates with God. The Father sends the Son. The Son reveals the Father. The Spirit continues this work through the church. When Jesus commissions His disciples, He is inviting them to participate in something that is already in motion.

This understanding shifts the weight of the mission. The responsibility of making disciples does not rest solely on human effort. It is rooted in the work that God has already accomplished. The role of the believer is to bear witness, to participate, and to remain faithful.

To understand how this plays out in practice, it is helpful to consider the foundational elements of discipleship. A disciple is first called before they are sent. In the Gospels, Jesus calls individuals to follow Him, inviting them into a relationship that would transform their lives. Fishermen left their nets. Others left their professions. They responded immediately, committing themselves to a new way of life.

Discipleship in this context was not simply about learning information. It was about becoming like the teacher. Rabbis in Jesus' time were respected not only for their knowledge, but for their way of life. Disciples followed closely, learning through both instruction and observation.

Jesus' disciples were more than students. They were apprentices. They walked with Him, listened to Him, and watched how He lived. Over time, they were shaped by His example and prepared to continue His work.

This pattern of discipleship can also be seen throughout Scripture. While the term "disciple" is not used in the Old Testament, the principle is present in relationships such as Moses and Joshua, and Elijah and Elisha. In each case, there is a transfer of knowledge, responsibility, and calling.

The early church built upon this foundation through what can be described as the spiritual DNA of discipleship. In Acts 2:42–47, we see a picture of this DNA in action. Believers devoted themselves to the apostles' teaching, to fellowship, to the breaking of bread, and to prayer. These were not optional practices. They were essential components of spiritual growth and community life.

The teaching of the apostles provided a foundation in the Word of God. Fellowship created a sense of belonging and mutual care. Sharing meals strengthened relationships and reinforced community. Prayer connected believers to God and to one another.

Together, these elements formed a pattern that could be replicated. Discipleship also carries a clear mandate. At the beginning of His ministry, Jesus called His disciples. At the end of His earthly ministry, He sent them. The command to make disciples is not a suggestion. It is a directive that applies to all believers.

This mandate includes a message, a mission, and a method. The message is the Gospel. The mission is to reach all people. The method includes going, baptizing, and teaching. Discipleship happens in the rhythm of everyday life, not just in structured environments.

It is a process. Jesus demonstrated this process through His own ministry. He taught, modeled, corrected, and encouraged. His disciples did not always understand. They struggled, questioned, and at times failed. Yet He continued to develop them, preparing them for the work ahead.

Discipleship requires growth, and growth often involves difficulty. There are moments when understanding is limited and faith feels weak. Yet even in those moments, the call remains the same: to follow. Transformation is at the heart of this process.

As Bill Hull writes, discipleship is not about producing stronger individuals, but about forming surrendered lives. Brandon Cook echoes this idea, emphasizing that transformation begins not with strength, but with honesty before God. It is in weakness, not perfection, that real change begins.

This reflects the teaching of Scripture. The Apostle Paul writes of boasting in weakness so that the power of Christ may be revealed. Jesus teaches that those who are poor in spirit are blessed. These teachings point to a Kingdom that operates differently from the world. Transformation is not immediate. It is a process that unfolds over time.

As Karline Fischer suggests, becoming more like Christ requires a movement away from self-centered living and toward a life led by the Spirit. A transformed life reflects truth, not personal preference. If the church is to have a meaningful impact, that impact must come from transformed lives.

Programs alone will not produce lasting change. True transformation occurs when individuals are changed from the inside out and live out their faith in authentic ways. The church is not called to function as a social organization, but as a community of people who have been transformed and are committed to living out that transformation.

This is where the conversation shifts into the present reality of virtual discipleship. During the pandemic, many churches were forced to adapt quickly. Worship services moved online. Bible studies became virtual. New forms of engagement emerged. In some cases, churches saw growth in ways they had not experienced before.

In conversations with others about their experiences during this time, one thing became clear. Churches were not only maintaining connection, they were reaching new people. Virtual membership began to grow, with individuals connecting from different cities and states. In one instance, a church shared how new members were fully integrated into the life of the congregation, even in a virtual setting. They were assigned class leaders and participated in the structures of the church as much as possible.

This raises important questions. What does membership look like in a virtual environment? How does the church disciple individuals who may never physically attend? How do practices such as baptism, communion, and community engagement function in this space?

These are not obstacles. They are opportunities. The ease of access provided by virtual platforms has allowed people who were previously unable to attend church due to work schedules, health limitations, or distance to now participate regularly. At the same time, this accessibility challenges the church to think beyond attendance and consider what true discipleship requires.

Being a disciple is more than watching a service or completing a form. It is about relationship, growth, and transformation. As one leader wisely noted, the question is not simply how to attract people, but how to sustain and disciple them once they arrive. The virtual world opens doors, but those doors must lead somewhere.

Some churches have already begun to explore solutions. Virtual class leaders have been appointed. Baptisms have been conducted when possible. Structures are being developed to support ongoing engagement.

Still, important questions remain. How will the church continue to nurture these relationships? How will it ensure that discipleship is not diluted in a virtual environment? How will it remain faithful to its theological foundation while embracing new methods?

These questions require thoughtful, intentional responses. The reality is that virtual discipleship is not a temporary solution. It is now a permanent part of the church's landscape. The challenge is not whether the church will engage in it, but how it will do so faithfully and effectively. The mission has not changed, but the context has, and the church must respond.

CHAPTER FOUR

Methodology

This book aims to equip not only DuPage AME Church but to equip all churches globally with a practical strategy for making disciples of non-traditional members who are worshipping virtually. It is grounded in the practice of living inquiry, which connects practice, ideas, and transformation within a church or community by engaging its members as co-researchers. The goal is to generate meaningful insight that leads to a usable model—one that can be applied not only in this context but in other churches as well.

This chapter outlines the qualitative approach used to shape the book and explains how information was gathered, evaluated, and applied. It also identifies the participants involved and describes the sessions that contributed to the development of a model designed to help any church effectively disciple non-traditional members in a virtual setting.

Qualitative Research

Churches must be willing to adapt their disciple-making approaches to reflect the realities of the current era. This book focuses on helping churches discover practical, virtual ways to engage people, understand their needs, build relationships, and guide them toward becoming committed followers of Christ.

The research for this book was conducted within the virtual congregational setting of DuPage AME Church. It focused on the lived experiences of both traditional and non-traditional members. Qualitative research relies on information gathered through observations, interviews, questionnaires, focus groups, and data collected through virtual platforms and church records. This type of research is not centered on numbers but on understanding experiences and meaning.

As outlined by Sharan Merriam, qualitative research includes several key characteristics: a focus on understanding meaning, the researcher serving as the primary instrument, the use of fieldwork, an inductive approach to analysis, and findings that are rich in description. These principles helped guide the development of this book.

Participants

The group involved seven individuals, including myself as the lead researcher and a professional associate who provided consultation and guidance. Participants were selected from DuPage AME Church and included both traditional and non-traditional members. Their involvement helped shape and test a strategy designed to equip individuals for the work of virtual disciple-making.

A focus group approach was used, where a small group of participants engaged in guided discussions around ministry challenges and opportunities. These sessions allowed for shared insight, reflection, and evaluation of the model being developed.

Professional Associate

To support this work, the late Bishop E. Anne Henning-Byfield served as a Professional Associate. She was the 135th elected and consecrated Bishop of the African Methodist Episcopal Church and the Presiding Prelate of the Sixteenth and the Thirteen Episcopal District of the African Methodist Episcopal Church. Her leadership spans multiple countries across the Caribbean, South America, and Europe. She also served as Chair of the Global Development Council, the Commission on Women in Ministry, and World Methodist Evangelism.

Bishop Byfield brought a strong academic and ministry background, including degrees from Wilberforce University, Newburgh Theological Seminary, Payne Theological Seminary, and Ashland Theological Seminary, along with an honorary doctorate from the R. R. Wright School of Religion in Johannesburg, South Africa. Her guidance was instrumental in shaping the direction of this work.

Context Associates

Two leaders from DuPage AME Church, one male and one female, were selected to serve as Context Associates. They played an active role in planning, implementing, and evaluating the ministry model presented in this book. Together, we discussed the focus of the work, identified the core challenges, and collaborated on strategies to reach the desired outcomes.

Ethnography

This work also incorporates an ethnographic approach, which involves engaging closely with a community to observe behavior, interactions, and patterns over time. Ethnography allows for a deeper understanding of how people experience ministry within their specific context.

Three core characteristics of a disciple were used as a foundation:

- One who is assured of their salvation (John 3:16)
- One who is growing in Christ (2 Peter)
- One who shares Christ's burden for others (Matthew 9:37)

Participants engaged in virtual Bible studies and worship services using platforms such as Facebook and Zoom. They attended three Bible study sessions and three worship services focused on understanding discipleship. Observations, questionnaires, and guided discussions were used to gather insight throughout the process.

These sessions also created space to emphasize the importance of disciple-making in everyday relationships—with family, friends, and colleagues—while exploring how this can be done effectively in virtual environments.

A post-session questionnaire was used to assess engagement, participation, and growth in understanding. Sermons and teaching moments reinforced biblical foundations, particularly the call in Matthew 28:19 to make disciples, while also introducing practical ways to connect and engage virtually.

Post-Session Questions and Discussion Prompts

Due to the limitations created by the pandemic, the group size remained small, with five active participants. The focus was not on demographic data but on experience and engagement.

A Likert Scale survey was used to measure responses to three post-session questions. In addition, opening discussion questions were used to understand participants' initial perspectives and track their growth throughout the process.

Question One

Post-session: How do you define evangelism?

Opening discussion: What has been your understanding and experience of evangelism and disciple-making prior to participating in these sessions?

Question Two

Post-session: Do you feel comfortable sharing your faith with others?

Opening discussion: Did anything shared during the sessions help deepen your understanding of evangelism and discipleship?

These questions were designed to help participants reflect on their understanding and begin applying what they learned in their personal lives.

Question Three

Post-session: Would you be able to teach someone else how to share their faith?

Opening discussion: After learning the characteristics of a disciple, what changes or insights have you experienced?

These discussions encouraged reflection, application, and personal growth.

Data Collection and Evaluation

Information was collected using digital tools and platforms, including social media, virtual services, and online Bible study sessions. Participants engaged using devices such as phones, tablets, and computers. Both live and recorded interactions contributed to the overall understanding of engagement and participation.

Further analysis of this information is presented in a later chapter.

Timeline

To ensure organization and consistency, a structured timeline was used to guide the process:

Week One

Introduction of the book's focus and selection of participants

Initial discussions on discipleship

Bible study session

Week Two

Observation of virtual worship and Bible study

Continued engagement

Week Three

Collection of participant feedback

Ongoing observation

Week Four

Continued participation and observation

Post-session responses collected

Week Five

Review and analysis of collected insights

Week Six

Final reflection and completion of written findings

CHAPTER FIVE

Field Experience

A significant amount of time and effort went into the design and development of this book. As a result of COVID-19, churches were forced to shift from traditional, in-person gatherings to virtual platforms. This shift created a new reality where people began connecting to the church virtual, and many of these individuals began to see themselves as members, even without physical attendance.

This book uses a qualitative approach, where the model was developed and evaluated simultaneously. The goal was to help non-traditional members become actively involved in the life of the church through virtual worship services and Bible study, ultimately leading them toward discipleship.

Data Collection Tools and Plan

Data Collection Tools

Several tools were used to gather meaningful insight:

- Focus Groups
  Participants were asked open-ended questions during Bible study sessions, allowing for discussion and reflection.
- Ethnography
  Participants engaged in the life of the church through virtual worship services, Sunday school, and Bible studies while observations and reflections were recorded.
- Post-Session Surveys (Likert Scale)
  Three questions were asked at the end of sessions using a five-point scale ranging from strong agreement to strong disagreement. These questions measured participants' confidence and understanding of evangelism.
  The primary platforms used included:
- Facebook Live (worship and Bible study)
- Zoom (worship and Bible study)
- Givelify (giving during worship services)

All data was collected electronically using digital devices, and participation occurred in real time.

Data Collection Process

To help non-traditional members become more engaged and grow spiritually, participants were invited to consistently attend virtual worship services and Bible studies.

The process began by establishing an online worship and Bible study environment to build a sense of community.

Over a three-month period, a consistent group of participants emerged. These individuals were identified as non-traditional members due to their regular participation in virtual services.

Once this core group was established, a key test was introduced. Participants were asked to pause their attendance for two weeks to observe whether non-traditional members would continue to attend and engage without them. This helped measure the strength and sustainability of the virtual community.

During this time:

- Non-traditional members continued attending services
- Engagement remained steady
- Giving patterns were observed
- Online interaction through comments and reactions continued

After the testing period, participants returned and evaluated the engagement levels of the non-traditional members.

Outcomes

Several important outcomes emerged:

- Non-traditional members became consistent participants in the life of the church
- They invited family, friends, and others through their social networks
- Services continued to grow through sharing and engagement

- Some participants began contributing financially

One of the most significant observations was that the church remained active and sustained through virtual participation alone. Even in the absence of traditional members, the services continued, and the Gospel continued to reach people.

This reinforced the truth found in Matthew 16:18—that the church will endure.

It also challenged a long-standing assumption: that church sustainability depends solely on in-person attendance and traditional giving patterns. This experience revealed that the church can continue to function, grow, and reach others through non-traditional members.

Participant Responses and Reflections

Participants were asked a series of questions to better understand their growth in evangelism and discipleship.

Question One

Participants initially expressed that they had little to no understanding of evangelism and were unclear on how to define it.

Question Two

Participants shared that, although they were introduced to the concepts of discipleship, they still did not feel fully confident in applying them. Many expressed a need for additional teaching and hands-on guidance.

Question Three

Participants again expressed uncertainty. However, through observation and discussion, it became clear that their hesitation was not due to lack of willingness, but lack of clarity and confidence.

This revealed an important insight: people are more likely to engage in evangelism when they clearly understand what it is and how to do it.

Observations

Throughout the virtual sessions, noticeable changes occurred:

- Increased participation and interaction
- Growth in relationships among participants
- Greater willingness to invite others
- Continued engagement through sharing and giving

Non-traditional members actively helped expand the reach of the church by consistently sharing services across their networks.

Survey Results (Likert Scale)

Across Facebook Live, Zoom, and Givelify platforms, results were consistent:

- Participants strongly disagreed that they could clearly define evangelism
- Participants strongly disagreed that they felt comfortable evangelizing
- Participants strongly disagreed that they could teach someone else how to evangelize

These results were consistent across all platforms, indicating a clear need for deeper teaching and practical training in evangelism.

Expanded Observations and Key Learnings

The overall goal of this book was to discover effective ways to incorporate non-traditional members into the life of the church through discipleship and virtual engagement. Based on the findings, the model proved to be effective and replicable across different church settings.

One challenge that surfaced involved older, traditional members who were initially uncomfortable with appearing on camera or using social media platforms. However, they were still willing to participate when given the option to engage at their own comfort level.

In additional congregational settings where this model was introduced, similar patterns emerged. One recurring question stood out:

"Can we keep some of our classes private?"

This question revealed a deeper concern about comfort, control, and unfamiliarity with virtual spaces. It also highlighted a tendency to unintentionally exclude non-traditional members.

Rather than rejecting the request, a balanced approach was introduced. Those who preferred private settings were encouraged to include someone from a younger generation—such as a grandchild, niece, nephew, or neighbor—who could help bridge the gap between traditional and virtual engagement.

This approach created:

- Intergenerational collaboration

- Increased comfort with technology
- Gradual exposure to public, virtual engagement

Over time, even those who were initially hesitant began to participate in live sessions in small ways, such as introducing lessons or summarizing discussions.

As confidence grew, so did participation.

Conclusion

This experience revealed that growth often begins with exposure, support, and patience. When individuals are given the space to learn, adapt, and engage at their own pace, they become more open to new methods of connection and discipleship.

The blending of traditional and non-traditional members created a stronger, more inclusive community. It allowed for broader discussions, deeper relationships, and a more expansive view of what it means to make disciples.

Ultimately, this process demonstrated that the church can evolve without losing its mission. By embracing new methods while remaining rooted in biblical truth, the church can continue to reach all people—fulfilling the call to "go… and make disciples of all nations."

CHAPTER SIX

Reflections, Summary, and Conclusions

In the New Testament, the final words of Jesus capture the heart of discipleship. In what is known as the Great Commission, Jesus says, *"All authority in heaven and on earth has been given to me. Go therefore and make disciples of all nations…"* (Matthew 28:18–20). This call is both clear and decisive. Jesus calls the disciple, but the disciple is also given a responsibility—to respond, to follow, and to help others do the same.

This book has focused on helping churches discover practical, virtual ways to minister, teach, and engage those who show up each week through virtual worship services, Bible studies, and other virtual spaces. These individuals—visitors, friends, family members, coworkers, and even strangers—represent what has been described as non-traditional members. As churches apply this model, they will begin to see these individuals become more engaged, more connected, and more active in the life of the church. Over time, that engagement leads to discipleship, and discipleship leads to multiplication.

The model presented in this book is designed to be adaptable and replicable. Churches of different sizes and contexts can apply these principles to guide their own efforts in virtual disciple-making.

Dietrich Bonhoeffer, in *Discipleship*, reflects on the calling of Matthew. When Jesus called him, Matthew did not hesitate or overanalyze the decision. He simply got up and followed. Bonhoeffer points out that this response may seem unreasonable by human standards. A more logical approach would have been to think through the decision, weigh the consequences, and then act. Yet Matthew's response was immediate obedience.

Discipleship, at its core, is not built on a system, a program, or a list of rules. It is built on following Jesus. It is not something one casually chooses from a set of life options. It is a response to a call—a call that comes from Christ Himself. Nothing should come between that call and the one who responds to it. My understanding of discipleship did not begin in theory. It began in experience.

As a child, I grew up attending St. Luke Baptist Church every Sunday with my family. There were times we stayed all day, moving from one service to the next, eating meals in between. What I did not realize at the time was that I was being shaped. The people in that church were not just attending services. They were actively nurturing my faith.

Looking back, I can clearly see that I was being discipled—consistently, intentionally, and over time. That experience stayed with me.

By the time I was ten or eleven years old, I had already begun sharing what I had learned with my friends in the neighborhood. I did not have formal training or structured language for it, but I was doing what I had seen modeled. I was beginning to make disciples in my own way.

Many of those childhood friends were eventually baptized. I remember one particular Sunday morning in July of 1972, standing near Deer Creek across from New Hope Missionary Baptist Church. It was a hot, sunny day, and we were baptized by full immersion. That moment was not just a memory. It was a continuation of a process that had already begun.

That experience shaped my belief: when people are nurtured consistently within a church community, (either way, whether it's the physical building or the virtual platform) they grow into confident disciples who, in turn, disciple others. This is how the cycle continues.

The opportunity to implement and test this model in multiple locations added depth to these findings. It also raised important questions about leadership, especially when stepping into new environments.

There were moments when I found myself wondering how to introduce a new way of worship and disciple-making into an established church setting. In those moments, the Holy Spirit provided clarity:

"When the Lord sends you to a new place, you do not need to fully understand how things have always been done. The Holy Spirit already knows. Your responsibility is to remain in tune, to be obedient, and to have the courage to act."

That guidance challenged a common belief—that leaders should wait before making changes. In many cases, waiting allows patterns to solidify, making change more difficult later. In my experience, implementing this approach early created momentum and openness.

That initial window—often referred to as the "honeymoon period"—is critical. During that time, people are more receptive, more curious, and more willing to engage. Introducing new approaches during this season allows for smoother integration and greater acceptance.

However, even with openness, there is often hesitation. One of the most important lessons learned is that people must first be willing to try something new. Without that initial willingness, progress cannot be made. Leadership, therefore, must focus on building trust, communicating clearly, and helping people see the value of the change.

At the same time, it is essential to meet people where they are. Not everyone will move at the same pace. Some will embrace change quickly, while others will need time to adjust. Creating space for both groups is key. This was especially evident in the virtual Sunday school settings, where a new approach to disciple-making began to take shape.

What emerged was not just a new method, but a new mindset. The shift to virtual engagement, accelerated by the pandemic push, revealed that the church is not confined to a building. It is a living, growing body that can function across spaces, platforms, and communities.

This is not a temporary adjustment. It is a transition. The Holy Spirit impressed upon me that this moment represents a new phase in how the church operates and how disciples are made. Leaders are not called to simply maintain what has always been done. They are called to help usher in what God is doing now.

For those entering new congregations, this responsibility is especially important. They are not sent to preserve systems, but to bring vision, direction, and growth. For those already established in their congregations, the opportunity still exists. The impact of the pandemic push has created a unique moment where change is not only possible but necessary. Many congregations are already aware that old methods alone are no longer sufficient.

This creates an opening. Sometimes the message must be spoken plainly: the church must be willing to release outdated approaches, embrace new opportunities, and remain committed to the mission of making disciples.

That mission has not changed. The method must.

BIBLIOGRAPHY

Adams, Jay E. *The Christian Counselor's New Testament and Proverbs*. Edited by Donn R. Arms. Fourth Revised Edition. Cordova, TN: Institute for Nouthetic Studies, 2019.

Althaus, Paul. *Der Geist der lutherischen Ethik im Augsburgischen Bekenntnis*. Munich: Chr. Kaiser, 1930.

Akin, Daniel. "How to Build a Theological Library." www.danielakin.com, 2013.

———. *Kirche und Volkskampf: Die Völkische Wille Im Licht des Evangeliums*. Gütersloh: C. Bertelsmann, 1928. *NL* 2 C 4.1b.

———. *Religiöser Sozialismus: Grundfragen der christlicher Sozialethik* (Religious socialism: Basic questions of Christian social ethics). Vol. 5, *Studien des apologetischen Seminars in Wernigerode* (Studies of the apologetics seminar in Wernigerode). Gütersloh: Bertelsmann, 1921. *NL* 4, 2.

Barry, J. D., Mangum, D., Brown, D. R., Heiser, M. S., Custis, M., Ritzema, E., … Bomar, D. 2012, 2016. *Faithlife Study Bible* (Ge 12:1–4). Bellingham, WA: Lexham Press.

Barth, Karl. *Der Römerbrief*. 2d ed. ed. Munich: Chr. Kaiser, 1923. English translation: *The Epistle to the Romans*.

Translated from the 6th German ed. by Edwin C. Hoskins. London, UK: Oxford University Press, 1933, 1960.

Bengel, Johann Albrecht. *Gnomon: Auslegung des Neuen Testamentes in fortlaufenden Anmerkungen.* Vol. 1, *Evangelien und Apostelgeschichte.* Published originally in Latin in 1742, German translation by C. F. Werner. Basel, 1876. [Uncorrected printing from the 3d ed., Berlin-Stuttgart, 1959.] English translation: *Gnomen of the New Testament.* Revised and edited by Andrew R. Fausset. 5 Vols. Philadelphia: Smith, English & Co., 1860.

Bergen, R. D. 2017. Genesis. In E. A. Blum & T. Wax Eds. *CSB Study Bible: Notes* Nashville, TN: Holman Bible Publishers.

Best, Ernest. *Disciples and Discipleship: Studies in the Gospel According to Mark.* Edinburgh: T&T Clark, 1986.

Bevans, Stephen B. *Models of Contextual Theology.* New York, NY: Orbis, 2006.

Bright, Bill. *Come Help Change the World.* San Bernardino, CA: Here's Life Publishers, 1979.

Brunner, Emil. *Das Gebot und die Ordnungen: Entwurf einer protestantisch theologischen Ethik.* Tübingen: Mohr (Paul Siebeck), 1932. *NL* 4, 6. English translation: *The Divine Imperative.* Translated by Olive Wyon. Philadelphia, PA: Westminster Press, 1947.

Der Mittler: Zur Besinnung über den Christusglauben. Tübingen: Mohr (Paul Siebeck), 1927. *NL* 3 B 15. English translation: *The Mediator.* Translated by Olive Wyon. New York, NY: Macmillan Press, 1934.

Byrley, C. (2014). Discipleship. D. Mangum, D. R. Brown, R. Klippenstein, & R. Hurst (Eds.). *Lexham Theological Wordbook*. Bellingham, WA: Lexham Press.

Bryson, John R., Lauren Andres, and Andrew Davies. 2020. COVID-19, virtual church Services and a New Temporary Geography of Home. *Tijdschrift Voor Economische En Sociale Geografie* 111, no. 3, (2020), 360-372. https://search-proquest-.com. Wilberforcepayne._idm.oclc.org/scholarly-journals/covid-19-virtual-church-services-new-temporary/docview/2421649068/se-2?accountid=191658.

Buckingham, Marcus. *One Thing You Need to Know.* New York, NY: Free Press, 2005.

Byrskog, Samuel. *Jesus the Only Teacher: Didactic Authority and Transmission in Ancient Israel, Ancient Judaism, and the Matthean Community*. Stockholm: Almqvist & Wiksell, 1994.

Chanda, Nayan. *Bound Together: How Traders, Preachers, Adventurers, and Warriors Shaped Globalization.* New Haven, CT: Yale University Press, 2007. https://search-proquest-com.wilberforcepayne.idm.oclc.org/books/bound-together/docview/2131364628/se-2?accountid=191658.

Comer, Gary Steven. *Soul Whisperer: Why the Church must Change the Way it Views Evangelism.* La Mirada, CA: Biola University, 2013. Order No. 3558332, In PROQUESTMS ProQuest Central, https://search-proquest-com.wilberforce payne.idm.oclc.org/docview/1348969935?accountid=191658.

Corbin, Juliet and Anselm Strauss. *Basics of Qualitative Research: Techniques and Procedures for Developing Grounded Theory.* Los Angeles, CA: Sage, 2008.

Digital Orthodoxy in the Post-Soviet World: The Russian Orthodox Church and Web 2.0. Edited by Mikhail Suslov andAndreas Umland. Berlin: Ibidem Verlag, 2016. https://search- proquest-com.wilberforcepayne.idm.oclc.org/books/digital- orthodoxy-post-soviet-world/docview/2236228183/se-2?accountid=191658.

Die Bekenntnisschriften der evangelisch-lutherischen Kirche. Vol. 1. Edited and published in the anniversary year of the Augsburg Confession. Göttingen: Vandenhoeck & Ruprecht, 1930. *NL*2C3. English translation: *The Book of Concord: The Confessions of the Evangelical Lutheran Church.* Edited and translated by Theodore G. Tappert, in collaboration with Jaroslav Pelikan, Robert H. Fischer, and Arthur C. Piepkorn. Philadelphia: Fortress Press, 1959.

Die Bibel oder die ganze Heilige Schrift des Alten und Neuen Testaments nach der deutschen Übersetzung D. Martin Luthers (The Bible or the entire Holy Scriptures of the Old and New Testaments according to the German translation of Dr. Martin Luther). Supervised by the Commission of the Deutsche Evangelische Kirchenkonferenz. Mitteloktav ed. Stuttgart, 1911. *NL*1A6.

Disciples - Oxford Biblical Studies Online. http://www.oxfordbiblicalstudies.com. wilberforcepayne.idm.oclc.org/article/opr/t94/e536?_hi=6&_pos=5 (accessed February 6, 2021.

Doan, Thien H. "*30-Day Evangelism Challenge: A Video-Based, Social Media-Driven Evangelism Training Program.*" Order No. 10281042. La Mirada, CA: Biola University, 2017. In PROQUESTMS ProQuest Central, https://search-proquest-com.wilberforce payne. idm. oclc.org/docview/1899924462?accountid=191658.

Dunn, James D. G. *Jesus Remembered.* Grand Rapids: Eerdmans, 2003. Longenecker, Richard N., ed. *Patterns of Discipleship in the New Testament.* Grand Rapids, MI: Eerdmans, 1996.

Eyre, Camilla. 2012. "From Social Butterfly to Engaged Citizen: Urban Informatics, Social Media, Ubiquitous Computing, and Mobile Technology to Support Citizen Engagement." *Social Alternatives* 31, no. 2: 52-53. https://search-proquest-com.wilberforcepayne.idm. oclc.org/scholarly-journals/social-butterfly-engaged-citizen-urban/docview/1442368023 /se-2?accountid=191658.

Galvan, Jose L. *Writing Literature Reviews: A Guide for Students of Social and Behavioral Sciences.* ISBN 10-193652337X.

Gittins, Anthony J. C. S. Sp. *The Way of Discipleship: Women, Men, and Today's Call to Mission.* (Collegeville, MN: Liturgical Press, 2016). https://search-proquest-com. wilberforcepayne.idm.oclc.org/books/way-discipleship/docview/2135415693/se-2?accountid=191658.

Gould, Meredith. *The Social Media Gospel: Sharing the Good News in New Ways*, 2nd ed. Collegeville, MN: Liturgical Press, 2015.

Hannah, John D. *The Kregel Pictorial Guide to Church History*, 6 vols. Grand Rapids, MI: Kregel, 2001–2011. Harrington, Daniel J. Gospel of Matthew. Oxford, UK: Oxford University Press, 2010). Accessed February 6, 2021. http://www.oxford bibliographies.com/display/id/obo-9780195393361-0078.

Hartman, D. 2016. *Church History for Modern Ministry: Why Our Past Matters for Everything We Do.* Bellingham, WA: Lexham Press.

Hill, Jonathan. Zondervan Handbook to the History of Christianity. Grand Rapids, MI: Zondervan, 2006.

Jackson, Jack. *Offering Christ. John Wesley's Evangelistic Vision* (Nashville, TN: Abingdon Press, 2017). Accessed December 28, 2020. ProQuest EBook Central.

Johnson, Jennifer. "With Religious Services Now Online, Music Helps Keep Worshipers at Home Connected to their Churches." TCA Regional News, May 14, 2020. https://search-proquest-com.wilberforcepayne.idm.oclc.org/wire-feeds/with-religious-services-now-online-music-helps/docview/2402563617/se-2?accountid=191658.

Kidner, D. 1967. *Genesis: An Introduction and Commentary*. Vol. 1. Downers Grove, IL: InterVarsity Press.

Luter, A. Boyd, Jr. "The Great Commission," *Edited by David Noel Freedman. The Anchor Yale Bible Dictionary.* New York, NY: Doubleday, 1992.

Luz, Ulrich. "The Disciples in the Gospel According to Matthew." *The Interpretation of Matthew* Edited by Graham Stanton; Philadelphia, PA: Fortress Press, 1983.

Madden, John and Dave Anderson. *Hey, Wait a Minute.* New York, NY: Ballantine, 1985.

Malphurs, Aubrey. *Developing a Vision for Ministry*, 3rd ed. Grand Rapids, MI: Baker Book Publisher, 2015.

Mathews, K. A. (2005). *Genesis 11:27–50:26*, Vol. 1B. Nashville, TN: Broadman & Holman Publishers.

Meier, John P. "The Circle of the Twelve: Did It Exist during Jesus' Public Ministry?" *Journal of Biblical Literature* 116 (1997): 635–72.

Morris, Leon. "The Gospel according to Matthew." *The Pillar New Testament Commentary.* Grand Rapids, MI; Leicester, England: W.B. Eerdmans; Inter-Varsity Press, 1992.

Nässelqvist, D. (2016). *Disciple.* In J. D. Barry, D. Bomar, D. R. Brown, R. Klippenstein, D. Mangum, C. Sinclair Wolcott, … W. Widder (Eds.), *The Lexham Bible Dictionary.* Bellingham, WA: Lexham Press.

Newman, Richard S. *Freedom's Prophet: Bishop Richard Allen, the AME Church, and the Black Founding Fathers.* 1st ed. (New York: NY: University Press, 2008). https://search-proquest-com.wilberforcepayne.idm.oclc.org/books/freedoms-prophet/docview/2131370758/se-2?accountid=191658.

Noll, Mark A. *Turning Points: Decisive Moments in the History of Christianity*. Grand Rapids, MI: Baker Academic, 2012.

Offen, Karl and Terry Rugeley, eds. *The Awakening Coast: An anthology of Moravian Writings from Eosquitia and Eastern Nicaragua, 1849-1899*2014 (Lincoln, NE: UNP – Nebraska). https://search-proquest-com.wilberforcepayne.idm.oclc. org/books/awakening-coast/ docview/2130925879/se-2?accountid=191658.

Oghogho, Julius. "Fostering Loving Relationships in Abundant Life Church in Croydon, Pennsylvania." *Dissertation* (Virginia Beach, VA: Regent University. 2020) Order No. 28031544. https://search-proquestcom.wilberforcepayne.idm.oclc .orgdissertations-theses/fostering-loving-relationships-abundant-life/docview/ 2446039544/se-2?accountid=191658. Coronavirus Research Database; ProQuest Central.

Overman, J. Andrew, "Disciple - Oxford Biblical Online." Accessed February 6, 2021. http://www. oxfordbiblicalstudies.com.wilberforcepayne.idm.oclc.org /article/opr/t120/e0194.

Plant, Stephen. *Bonhoeffer: Outstanding Christian Thinkers. London*. Bloomsbury Publishing Plc, 2004. Accessed March 28, 2021. ProQuest Ebook Central.

Rea, Robert F. *Why Church History Matters: An Invitation to Love and Learn from Our Past.* Downes Grove, IL: InterVarsity Press, 2014.

Rengstorf, Karl Heinrich. "Μαθητής (*Mathētēs*)." In *Theological Dictionary of the New Testament* IV. 1992.

Rhoads, David, Joanna Dewey, and Donald Michie. *Mark as Story: An Introduction to the Narrative of a Gospel.* 2nd ed. Minneapolis, MN: Fortress Press, 1999.

Ryan, Rosalie. "The Women from Galilee and Discipleship in Luke." *Biblical Theology Bulletin* 15 (1985): 56–59.

Sanders, E. P. *The Historical Figure of Jesus.* London: Penguin Books, 1995. Segovia, Fernando F., ed. *Discipleship in the New Testament.* Philadelphia: Fortress Press, 1985.

Smith, Fred. *Learning to Lead.* Waco, TX: Word Books, 1986.

Sprinkle, Preston. *Go: Returning Discipleship to the Front Lines of Faith*, NavPress Publishing Group, 2016. *ProQuest Ebook Central*, https://search-proquest-com.wilberforcepayne.idm.oclc.org/legacydocview/ EBC/5395830?accountid =191658.

Stringer, Earnest T., ed. *Community-Based Ethnography: Breaking Traditional Boundaries of Research, Teaching, and Learning* (Mahwah, UK: Lawrence Erlbaum Associates, 1997).

The Book of Concord. Die Bekenntnisschriften der evangelisch-lutherischen Kirche. Bornhäuser, Karl Bernhard. *Die Bergpredigt: Versuch einer zeitgenössischen Auslegung* (The Sermon on the Mount: An essay toward a contemporary interpretation). Gütersloh: Bertelsmann, 1927. *NL* 1 D 2.

Tucker, Ruth. *Parade of Faith: A Biographical History of the Christian Church.* Grand Rapids, MI: Zondervan, 2011.

Valentine Low, The Times" Virtual Church Services Reach Masses" London (UK) [London (UK)]23 Mar 2020: 10. Accessed November 28, 2020.

https://search-proquestcom.wilberforcepayne. idm. oclc.org/ docview/2381540486/3C3CD 45E72E749F0PQ/7?accountid= 191658.

Walton, Robert C. *Chronological and Background Charts of Church History*. Grand Rapids, MI: Zondervan, 2005.

Wanner, Catherine. 2011. Communities of the Converted: Ukrainians and Global Evangelism. Ithaca: Cornell University Press. https://search-proquestcom. wilberforcepayne. idm. oclc.org/ books/ communities-converted/docview/ 2131964638/se-2?accountid=191658.

Weder, Hans. "Disciple, Discipleship." Edited by David Noel Freedman. Translated by Dennis Martin. *The Anchor Yale Bible Dictionary*. New York: Doubleday, 1992.

Wilkins, Michael J. *The Concept of Disciple in Matthew's Gospel: As Reflected in the Use of Μαθητής (Mathētēs)*. Leiden: Brill, 1988.

www.ingramcontent.com/pod-product-compliance
Lightning Source LLC
Chambersburg PA
CBHW022120050726
47591CB00002B/872
* 9 7 8 1 9 6 8 0 9 2 7 9 5 *